Learning to read. Reading to learn!

LEVEL ONE Sounding It Out   Preschool–Kindergarten
For kids who know their alphabet and are starting to sound out words.

learning sight words • beginning reading • sounding out words

LEVEL TWO Reading with Help   Preschool–Grade 1
For kids who know sight words and are learning to sound out new words.

expanding vocabulary • building confidence • sounding out bigger words

LEVEL THREE Independent Reading   Grades 1–3
For kids who are beginning to read on their own.

introducing paragraphs • challenging vocabulary • reading for comprehension

LEVEL FOUR Chapters   Grades 2–4
For confident readers who enjoy a mixture of images and story.

reading for learning • more complex content • feeding curiosity

Ripley Readers Designed to help kids build their reading skills and confidence at any level, this program offers a variety of fun, entertaining, and unbelievable topics to interest even the most reluctant readers. With stories and information that will spark their curiosity, each book will motivate them to start and keep reading.

Vice President, Licensing & Publishing Amanda Joiner
Editorial Manager Carrie Bolin

Editor Jessica Firpi
Writer Korynn Wible-Freels
Designer Mark Voss
Reprographics Bob Prohaska

Published by Ripley Publishing 2020

10 9 8 7 6 5 4 3 2 1

Copyright © 2020 Ripley Publishing

ISBN: 978-1-60991-345-8

No part of this publication may be reproduced in whole or in part, stored in a retrieval system, or transmitted in any form by any means, electronic, mechanical, photocopying, recording, or otherwise, without written permission from the publisher.

For more information regarding permission, contact:
VP Licensing & Publishing
Ripley Entertainment Inc.
7576 Kingspointe Parkway, Suite 188
Orlando, Florida 32819

Email: publishing@ripleys.com
www.ripleys.com/books
Manufactured in China in January 2020.

First Printing

Library of Congress Control Number: 2019954287

PUBLISHER'S NOTE
While every effort has been made to verify the accuracy of the entries in this book, the Publisher cannot be held responsible for any errors contained in the work. They would be glad to receive any information from readers.

PHOTO CREDITS

5 (c) © Public Domain {{PD–US}} "The boy travellers in the Russian empire: adventures of two youths in a journey in European and Asiatic Russia, with accounts of a tour across Siberia", Thomas Wallace Knox (1886), pp. 198, New York: Harper & brothers, https://archive.org/stream/boytravellersinr00knox/boytravellersinr00knox#page/198/mode/1up; **6** © Public Domain {{PD-US}} "Switchback Railroad, Mauch Ch Pa." (Source Imprint: 1859-1885?), image is available from the New York Public Library's Digital Library under the digital ID G91F347_039F; **24–25** © Public Domain {{PD–US}} Bhakta Dano. Original uploader was Oldane at en.wikipedia; **28–29** © Dusso Janladde, Wikimedia Commons//CC BY–SA 3.0; **30–31** © Jazon88, Wikime Commons//CC BY–SA 3.0

All other photos are from Shutterstock.com

Key: t = top, b = bottom, c = center, l = left, r = right, sp = single page, dp = double page, bkg = background

LEXILE®, LEXILE FRAMEWORK®, LEXILE ANALYZER®, the LEXILE® logo and POWERV® are trademarks of MetaMetrics, Inc., and are registered in the United States and abroad. The trademark and names of other companies and products mentioned herein are the property of their respective owners. Copyright © 2019 MetaMetrics, Inc. All rights reserved.

Ripley Readers
Roller Coasters

All true and unbelievable!

a Jim Pattison Company

Ever wonder how roller coasters got their start?

Before Six Flags and Disney World, there were giant ice hills 70 feet tall!

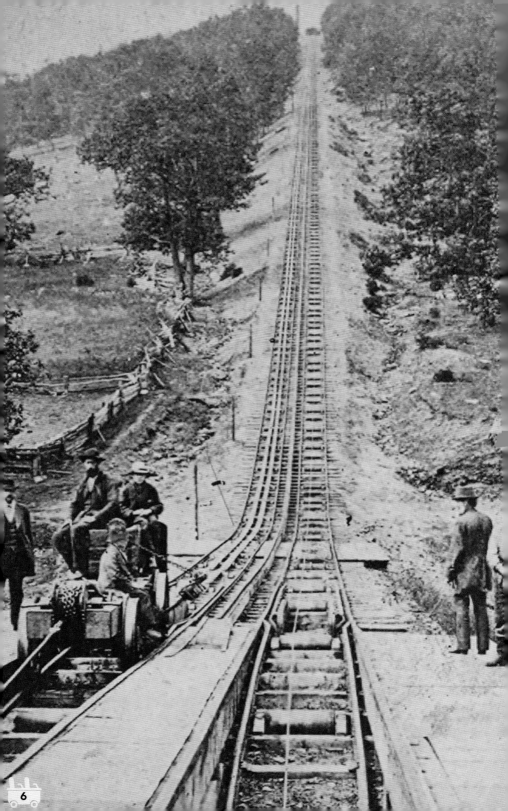

People long ago found neat ways to make roller coasters.

The first one in America was a railroad track going down a hill!

The oldest ones were made from wood. You can still ride the Cyclone at Coney Island, which was made in 1927!

Some rides pull you up the hill with a chain.

Others store energy and launch you up fast!

Brakes slow you down on the curves and stop you when the ride is over.

The brakes are on the track, not on the car!

A coaster car gathers energy as it goes up a hill.

That energy keeps the car moving the rest of the ride!

G force is the push you feel on your body as you speed up!

Can you feel your back push against the seat?

Have you ever felt yourself lift off the chair?

During air time, your organs float around inside of you!

That much speed makes you stronger than gravity!

Don't worry, you will not fall out on the big, round loops!

Steel coasters have more loops and turns than wooden ones.

Do you like to sit, stand, or dangle on a ride?

This coaster is a living legend! Leap the Dips was made in 1902 and only goes 10 miles an hour! There are not even seatbelts!

A ride on the Steel Dragon is worth the wait.

Many rides are only two minutes long. This one is four!

Would you ride this king of coasters?

The Kingda Ka is 456 feet tall! That is taller than the Statue of Liberty!

Do you have a need for speed? The Formula Rossa is the fastest ride in the world!

Ripley Readers

All true and unbelievabl[e]

Ready for More?

Ripley Readers feature unbelievable but true facts and stories!

For more information about Ripley's Believe It or Not!, go to www.ripleys.com